W9-CNA-366

GAME DAY

VIP PASS

TO A

PRO BASKETBALL

GAME DAY

FROM THE LOCKER ROOM TO THE PRESS BOX

[AND EVERYTHING IN BETWEEN]

by Clay Latimer

Consultant:
Joe Schmit
Sports Director, KSTP-TV
St. Paul, Minnesota

CAPSTONE PRESS
a capstone imprint

Sports Illustrated KIDS Game Day is published by Capstone Press,
151 Good Counsel Drive, P.O. Box 669, Mankato, Minnesota 56002.
www.capstonepub.com

Copyright © 2011 by Capstone Press, a Capstone imprint.
All rights reserved.
No part of this publication may be reproduced in whole or in part,
or stored in a retrieval system, or transmitted in any form or by any means,
electronic, mechanical, photocopying, recording, or otherwise, without
written permission of the publisher.
For information regarding permission, write to Capstone Press,
151 Good Counsel Drive, P.O. Box 669, Dept. R, Mankato, Minnesota 56002.

Sports Illustrated Kids is a trademark of Time Inc. Used with permission.

Books published by Capstone Press are manufactured with paper
containing at least 10 percent post-consumer waste.

Library of Congress Cataloging-in-Publication Data
Latimer, Clay, 1952–
    VIP pass to a pro basketball game day: from the locker room to the press box
(and everything in between) / by Clay Latimer.
    p. cm.—(Sports Illustrated KIDS. Game day.)
    Includes bibliographical references and index.
    Summary: "Describes various activities and people who work behind the
scenes during a National Basketball Association game"—Provided by publisher.
    ISBN 978-1-4296-5463-0 (library binding)
    ISBN 978-1-4296-6284-0 (paperback)
1. Basketball—Juvenile literature. 2. National Basketball Association—Juvenile
literature. I. Title. II. Series.
GV885.1.L38 2011
796.323'64—dc22   2010032209

Editorial Credits
Aaron Sautter, editor; Ted Williams, designer; Eric Gohl,
    media researcher; Eric Manske, production specialist

Photo Credits
Corbis/Mark Peterson, 26
Getty Images Inc./NBAE/Andrew D. Bernstein, 10; Garrett W. Ellwood, 6;
    Rocky Widner, 23
Shutterstock/Steve Cukrov, background (basketball court)
Sports Illustrated/Bob Rosato, cover, 13; Chuck Solomon, 9; Damian
    Strohmeyer, 16, 25; Jeffery A. Salter, 22; John W. McDonough, 4, 12,
    17, 18, 21, 28, 29; Robert Beck, 11, 15

Design Elements
Shutterstock/bioraven; Daniela Illing; Iwona Grodzka;
    Marilyn Volan; Zavodskov Anatoliy Nikolaevich

Printed in the United States of America in Stevens Point, Wisconsin.
092010   005934WZS11

TABLE OF CONTENTS

SEP 2 6 2011

National Basketball Association (NBA) games are packed with action. But the excitement doesn't just happen on the court. Another thrilling world exists behind the scenes. Behind every slam dunk looms a hard-working coach. Production crews work many hours to prepare exciting **halftime** shows. During road trips, equipment managers make sure the players have the supplies they need.

To understand the big picture, you have to look inside the locker rooms and training rooms around the league. How do teams travel to games? How do referees prepare for games? How does the entertainment crew create a fun atmosphere? There's much more to a basketball game than just shooting and dribbling the ball.

halftime—a short break in the middle of a game

SPORTS FACT

The NBA was created on June 6, 1946, in New York City. At that time it was called the Basketball Association of America. The first official game was played between the New York Knicks and Toronto Huskies. The Knicks won, 68–66.

UP AND AWAY

It is midnight as the Los Angeles Lakers' plane reaches cruising altitude. It's the fourth day of an eight-game road trip. The team is tired and bleary-eyed. During the NBA season, players often get only one day of rest between games. It can be an exhausting grind.

Players eat well and relax during flights between games.

But at least the teams travel in style. Their plane is specially designed to provide comfort for big men. Every other row of seats is removed to create plenty of legroom. Players can fully recline their seats to turn them into temporary beds. A few players may sink into a cushy couch at the back of the plane.

During the flight, the coaches watch game film of the team's next opponent in first class. Players often enjoy playing cards, watching a movie, or listening to music. Flight attendants also serve large meals of fine foods and desserts.

The players continue to live in style even after the plane lands. They hop on a bus and are whisked to a fancy hotel. Each player gets his own room with plenty of comforts.

■ TAKING CARE OF HIS FEET

When they step on the court, players have to rely on their feet. Houston Rockets forward Shane Battier wears slippers off the court. "My feet are my livelihood, so I need to keep them happy," he says. "I probably wear these six or seven hours a day. They're very soft, and they don't make my feet sweat too much."

ANOTHER DAY, ANOTHER CITY

In their hotel rooms, NBA players roll out of bed. It's 9:00 in the morning, and it's time to go to work. After breakfast the team boards a bus for the arena. When the players get to their locker room, they watch film of the opposing team. A coach then gives a scouting report. He tells the players about their opponent's style of play. He reminds them what they need to keep in mind for the game.

The players then head to the court for the morning shoot-around. During this light one-hour practice, the players work on their game plan. They focus on the opponent's playing style and practice the best defense to use in the game. They also work on their own offensive plays so they can score quickly and often.

As practice ends, several players move to midcourt for a long-range shooting contest. Meanwhile, the coaches are all business. They'll soon begin another series of meetings to discuss strategies for the upcoming game.

After the morning practice, players are given the afternoon off. Some use the personal time to visit a school or hospital to do charity work. Shopping malls are also popular places to go. Other players like to catch a movie at a nearby theater.

After a few hours, players return to their hotel rooms. Some might take a nap. Others relax while watching TV. Then they'll take a quick shower and head back to the arena. By game time they'll be physically and mentally ready to play at their best.

At the morning shoot-around, players and coaches practice plays and strategies for the upcoming game.

THE COUNTDOWN

Before the opening tipoff, the locker rooms are buzzing hives of activity. The busiest place is the **trainer's** room. Players stream in and out to get ankles taped to help avoid injuries. Some players might have sore joints checked and rubbed down. Players each get ready for the game in their own way. Some are serious and businesslike. Others like to listen to music or joke around to calm their jittery nerves.

trainer—a person who helps athletes get in the best physical condition to compete in a sports event

Players each have their own locker room routine to prepare for a game.

Warm-up exercises and practice drills are important to help avoid injuries.

As fans start to fill the seats, both teams go through warm-ups on the court. The players do stretching exercises, jog through **layup** drills, and practice dribbling and shooting. Soon they head back to their locker rooms. It's time to meet with their coaches to go over any last minute game plans.

layup—a close shot where the ball is gently played off the backboard and into the hoop

During introductions, players often cheer on their teammates as they charge onto the court.

Loud music soon starts thumping in the arena. The announcer begins pumping up the crowd. The players line up to run onto the court when their names are called. They wave to the crowd and head toward their bench. It's time to play ball!

■ STRANGE ROUTINES

Many NBA players are superstitious. They feel they must follow the same routine before every game. LeBron James uses a special handshake for each of his teammates. He goes through them all, one at a time, before every game. Chris Paul says the same prayer, listens to the same songs, and high-fives the assistant equipment manager before every game. Rasual Butler always dresses left to right and takes five sips of his drink before entering a game. Kevin Garnett eats a peanut butter and jelly sandwich before each game.

READY FOR SOME FUN

On game day, an NBA arena is bustling with activity. Fans can buy T-shirts, hats, and other souvenirs with team logos. At courtside, they watch for players to emerge for warm-ups—hoping to get a star's autograph.

Once the game starts, fans stand at their seats for a better view. They often yell, stomp their feet, or boo opposing players. Behind the opponent's basket, fans wave and spin pinwheels to distract free-throw shooters.

During pauses in the game, cameras sometimes zoom in on the fans. Fans can watch the video screen to see themselves or a neighbor waving at the crowd. Meanwhile, streams of fans flow to concession stands to buy everything from pizza to ice cream to tacos. They then hurry back to their seats. Nobody wants to miss the next big shot.

SPORTS FACT

In 2010 a total of 108,713 fans attended the NBA All-Star game at Cowboys Stadium in Texas. It was the biggest crowd ever for a basketball game.

CELEBRITY FANS

One of the Los Angeles Lakers' most loyal fans is actor Jack Nicholson. He has had courtside seats for nearly 30 years and attends almost every home game. Like all Lakers fans, actor Leonardo DiCaprio likes to cheer loudly for the team. "Well, he sits right behind my wife and they get a little rowdy," guard Kobe Bryant said. "He really gets into the game. They're pretty passionate fans, so that's always good."

THE SHOW BEGINS

The starters peel off their warm-up outfits and walk onto the floor. Cheerleaders line up in front of the fans to begin their routines. An official tosses the ball high, and the game is on—for the entertainment crew. The arena's production crew works hard to keep people entertained throughout the game.

SPORTS FACT

During a typical Chicago Bulls game, fans consume 2,800 slices of pizza and 3,500 hot dogs. Workers remove up to 10 tons (9 metric tons) of trash after every home game.

Something is always happening during a game. A master of ceremonies (MC) runs contests for the crowd. The MC also introduces celebrities who might be sitting at courtside. Dance teams perform routines while mascots throw T-shirts into the stands. A mini blimp might fly over the crowd to drop souvenirs to the fans.

Preparing all the fun is hard work. An entertainment director lines up music and video clips before the season begins. During every home game, the director makes sure everybody follows the plans to keep the fans entertained.

Team mascots often thrill fans with amazing slam dunks during timeouts and halftime shows.

THE HEALING TOUCH

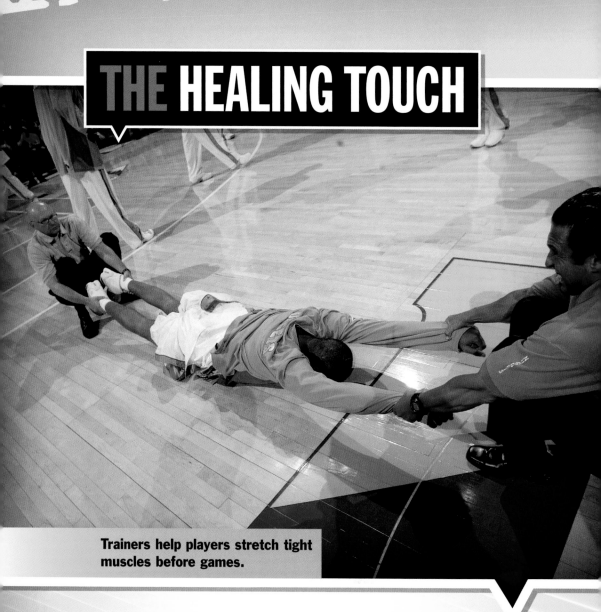

Trainers help players stretch tight muscles before games.

A lone figure sits in the visitor's locker room, preparing for another game. He's confident, relaxed, and talented. But he's not a player. He's an NBA trainer. His job is to try to prevent player injuries and treat any that do happen.

Athletic trainers often spend more time with players than the coaches. They work hard before, during, and after games to keep players healthy. Before the players take the court, they tape ankles, give light massages, and apply ointments. As the game is played, they continually scan the court, hoping the players avoid injuries. When injuries do occur, trainers work with the team doctors to treat them quickly. After the game, trainers soothe injured knees and rub cramped muscles.

▮ STAYING HEALTHY

Few players work as hard to keep themselves healthy as LeBron James. He gets massages on most game days. He also gets his ankles heavily taped. James even wears a padded vest under his jersey to protect his ribs. After a game, he ices his feet and lower back. But he doesn't stop there. Like several NBA players, he also practices yoga. Yoga helps players gain strength, flexibility, and better control over their bodies.

ORDER ON THE COURT

Just two minutes into the game, the coach stands up. "Call the foul!" he yells at a referee. "Why don't you call the foul?" The ref pays no attention. It's just a normal day for him. Being an NBA referee often means being criticized and booed.

Officials take their jobs seriously. On game day the three-man crew goes over film of both teams. Referees want to be familiar with the players' moves and style of play. They need to be ready if players use any illegal moves during the game. Then it's time to head to the arena.

▪ BREAKING NEW GROUND

Violet Palmer was the first woman to officiate a major U.S. professional sport. She made her NBA debut on October 31, 1997. Since then she has officiated at more than 700 regular-season games and four playoff games. "As the years went on, the players and coaches realized that I'm just one of the guys," Palmer said. "If you can do your job, you're going to earn the respect of the players and coaches."

Coaches sometimes strongly disagree
with an official's calls during games.

When they arrive, the referees loosen up
with stretching exercises. Then they discuss the
lineups and **matchups**. They want to be as
prepared as possible to call the game accurately.

lineup—the list of players participating
in a game and their positions

matchup—the pairing of two opposing
athletes for a sporting contest

HALFWAY THROUGH

Halftime allows trainers to stretch and rub out players' cramped muscles.

As the first half ends, both teams quickly head to their locker rooms. But it's not time to rest. It's time to make adjustments and change strategy for the second half. Halftime gives teams only 15 minutes, so they have to move fast.

In the locker room, injured players head to the trainer's room to treat twisted ankles or cramped muscles. The rest of the team grabs energy drinks and discusses what happened in the first half.

Meanwhile, the coaches hold a quick meeting in their office. They look for ways to improve the team's performance. They might adjust their offensive attack with more fast breaks. Or they might find a way to tighten up the defense. Maybe using more man-to-man coverage will help stop the other team.

After the five-minute meeting, the head coach gathers the team. He explains the changes planned for the second half. He draws out plays on a whiteboard to show the changes to the players. Then it's time to head back to keep battling for the win.

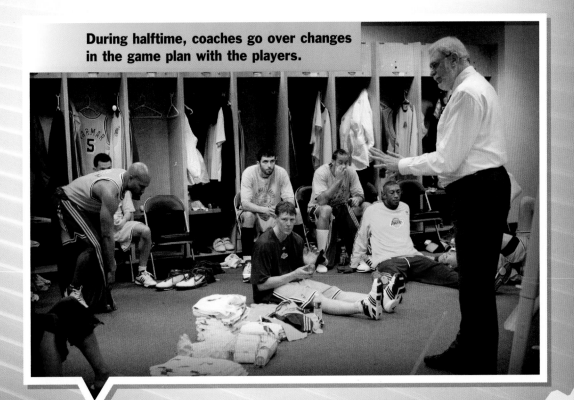

During halftime, coaches go over changes in the game plan with the players.

CALLING THE SHOTS

Coaches spend hours creating a game plan for every game. They scout the opposing team and study film from previous games. They decide on the best offensive plays to score points. They choose the best defensive style to keep the other team from scoring.

Like the players on the court, each assistant coach has a specific role during the game. One assistant keeps track of every possession. If the team hasn't scored for a while, he reminds the head coach how they scored their last basket. "We should try that play again," he says.

Another assistant coach watches how players are shooting. "You're off balance!" he yells when one player misses a jump shot. During a timeout, he tells another, "Try a head fake to move the defender off of you."

When the game is on the line, the coaches call a crucial timeout. The players catch their breath while the coaches huddle together. They discuss possible plays that may help them score. When they decide what to do, the head coach gathers the players together and outlines the plan. By following his instructions, the team may end up getting the win.

During timeouts, coaches gather players together to discuss important plays.

SPECIAL EDITION

For reporters and **journalists**, the basketball arena is their office. They work long hours to keep the fans informed. Journalists usually arrive at least two hours before game time. They often talk with players and coaches before the game begins.

journalist—someone who writes news stories

Reporters get a great view of the game from the press box.

As the game progresses, a newspaper reporter jots down notes and posts **blogs** on his paper's Web site. When the game is over, he rushes to the locker room to interview players and coaches. Then he writes the story of the game. He files the story with the newspaper long after the fans have left.

Radio play-by-play announcers spend a lot of time with the team. They tape interviews to play during game-day broadcasts. But their primary job is to describe the games for listeners at home.

TV broadcasters work nonstop to inform fans about their favorite teams and players. A TV crew prepares player profiles and team stories to broadcast before the game and at halftime. During the game, the play-by-play announcer describes the action on the court. Meanwhile, the color analyst explains the strategies that the coaches are using.

blog—a type of online diary that other people can read on the Internet

SPORTS FACT

In 2007 more than 100 million Chinese people watched a live broadcast of an NBA game. The game matched Houston Rockets star Yao Ming against Milwaukee Bucks rookie Yi Jianlian. It was the first time the two Chinese stars faced one another.

CALLING IT A NIGHT

After the final buzzer, players often congratulate each other for a well-played game.

After the game, the opposing teams shake hands and head to their locker rooms. One player limps into the trainer's room to treat his twisted ankle. Another player looks at a stat sheet to see his final rebound total. The sound of hissing showers lingers in the background. Soon the doors open and reporters stream in. They want to interview star players who made key plays of the game.

Reporters often interview key players when a game is over.

Another night in the NBA drags to a close. Long lines of traffic crawl out of parking lots. Cheerleaders, production crews, mascots, and others have worked hard all day to entertain the fans. In a couple of days, many of them will return for another game and another day of NBA fun.

HELPING THOSE IN NEED

Many NBA players are involved with charity work. Former center Dikembe Mutombo worked for years to build a hospital in his hometown in Africa. Steve Nash and The Steve Nash Foundation give time and money to help neglected and abused children. The Phoenix Suns' star guard also paid for building part of a hospital in Paraguay.

GLOSSARY

blog (BLOG)—a type of online diary that other people can read on the Internet

halftime (HAF-time)—a short break in the middle of a game

journalist (JUR-nuh-list)—someone who collects information and writes news stories for newspapers, magazines, TV, or radio

layup (LAY-uhp)—a close shot where the ball is gently played off the backboard and into the hoop

lineup (LINE-uhp)—the list of players participating in a game and their positions

mascot (MASS-kot)—an animal, person, or thing that represents a team

matchup (MACH-uhp)—the pairing of an offensive player against a defensive player for a sporting contest

trainer (TRAY-nur)—a person who treats athletes' injuries and helps them get in the best physical condition to compete in a sports event

READ MORE

Fawaz, John. *High-Flying Stars.* New York: Scholastic Inc., 2007

Fawaz, John. *Megastars 2008.* New York: Scholastic Inc., 2008.

Shea, Therese. *Basketball Stars.* Sports Stars. New York: Children's Press, 2007.

INTERNET SITES

FactHound offers a safe, fun way to find Internet sites related to this book. All of the sites on FactHound have been researched by our staff.

Here's all you do:

Visit *www.facthound.com*

Type in this code: 9781429654630

 Check out projects, games and lots more at www.capstonekids.com

INDEX